KINGFISHER
LONDON & NEW YORK

KINGFISHER
LONDON & NEW YORK

Text and illustration copyright © Macmillan Publishers International Ltd 2024
First published in 2024 in the United States by Kingfisher
120 Broadway, New York, NY 10271
Kingfisher is an imprint of
Macmillan Children's Books, London
All rights reserved

Distributed in the U.S. and Canada by Macmillan,
120 Broadway, New York, NY 10271

Library of Congress Cataloging-in-Publication Data has been applied for

ISBN 978-0-7534-8063-2

This book is not authorized, licensed, or endorsed by Taylor Swift or any affiliate.

Kingfisher books are available for special promotions and premiums.
For details contact: Special Markets Department, Macmillan,
120 Broadway, New York, NY 10271

For more information, please visit
www.kingfisherbooks.com

Printed in China
2 4 6 8 9 7 5 3 1

EU representative: 1st Floor, The Liffey Trust Centre,
117-126 Sheriff Street Upper, Dublin 1 D01 YC43

Let's Meet
TAYLOR

ILLUSTRATED BY MARIANA AVILA LAGUNES
WRITTEN BY ALEXANDRA KOKEN AND CLAIRE BAKER

On a winter's day in 1989, Scott and Andrea Swift welcomed their new baby girl and named her Taylor.

The music-loving parents named her after one of their favorite singers.

Little Taylor's grandmother was an opera singer,
so music was a big part of her life
ever since she was little.

Animal-loving Taylor had a magical childhood.
She grew up on a Christmas tree farm in Pennsylvania.

It was the perfect place for Taylor to ride
horses, play with her younger brother,
Austin—and to daydream!

She enjoyed making up
stories and rhymes, too.

Just like her grandmother, Taylor loved singing. She took acting classes and enjoyed performing in musicals in her hometown theater.

Taylor had fun writing poems, too.

She even won a national poetry competition when she was just ten years old.

Taylor's parents were very proud of her, but they knew she had one dream that was bigger than any other. She wanted to be a country singer.

To help make Taylor's dream come true, they took her on trips to Nashville, Tennessee, the home of country music.

Taylor spoke to every record company
she could. She sang them well-known
country songs but nobody gave
her a record deal.

So Taylor headed back home,
but she wasn't going to give up!

Taylor knew she had to change something to be noticed.

She decided she wouldn't sing the same songs as other country music stars anymore. She would only sing new songs, ones that she wrote herself.

Taylor's ♥ Songs

So Taylor learned how to play the guitar.
Then she was ready to write her own songs.
One of them was about a girl
who dares to be different.

That song was called "Lucky You."

Now Taylor was even more determined to be a singer.

She listened to country music's biggest stars over and over, practicing the guitar until her fingers hurt...

...and performing everywhere she could—at festivals, games, and sometimes in coffee shops.

By her thirteenth birthday, Taylor knew she could make it. Thirteen was her lucky number after all!

Taylor's parents thought so, too, so the Swift family made a huge decision. They moved close to Nashville.

Now Taylor was really excited! By performing in Nashville more often, she was sure she could win over the record companies there.

And she did! By the time she was fourteen, Taylor had signed a record deal to write her own songs at last. Her dream was starting to come true.

Taylor got right to work writing and performing her own songs. Once she had signed a new contract, she began recording her first album.

The album was a huge success and
Taylor was one of the youngest singers
ever to win a country music award.

But there was still
so much more she
wanted to do and
a lot more music
she wanted
to share.

As Taylor recorded more songs, her
fans enjoyed watching her perform
her music at concerts all
over the world.

She always likes to make her shows bright,
colorful, and full of surprises for her fans.

It's fun to watch Taylor change her outfit for almost every song, too.

lilac beads

no sleeves

full skirt

As Taylor got older, she wasn't afraid to try out other styles of music. Some people thought she should only sing country songs, but Taylor really wanted to try something new.

She started performing pop and folk songs. Everyone loved them!

Whatever style of song she writes, Taylor knows it has to mean something to her and come from her heart.

Taylor's fans are called Swifties and she has always tried really hard to make them feel extra special.

24

Sometimes she hides little surprises for them to find in her songs, videos, and messages.

Swifties think of Taylor like a bit of a special friend, even though most of them have never actually met her.

Now she's all grown up, Taylor still loves animals. Her three pet cats, Meredith Grey, Olivia Benson, and Benjamin Button, have even appeared in one of her music videos.

They're almost as famous as Taylor herself!

At home, Taylor likes to cook, bake, and
watch movies, just like many of her fans.
She still hangs out with her family and
friends when she can, too.

Taylor often uses her fame to encourage everyone to be the best they can be. She tells us how important it is to be strong, kind, and think of other people.

Most of all, Taylor makes sure she does things her way so that she can keep creating the music she wants to make.

Talented Taylor doesn't just sing and write songs!
From acting in movies to directing her own music videos,
Taylor always tries her very best, no matter what she does.

Even when things are tough, she remembers how strong she can be—and she inspires her fans to never give up on their dreams either.

That's why people all over the world love Taylor and her music!